The Oz Guitar

A Beginner's Guide to Popular Music

MW01195496

Table of Contents

The Oz Guitar Method:

A Beginner's Guide to Popular Music

Acknowledgements

Special thanks to: Shellie Terry, formatting and layout; Deanna Salt Media, photography; Terzian Productions, videography; USF Innovative Education Lab; USF School of Music; Patel Conservatory; Del Couch Music Education Foundation; & F-flat Books.
TAYLOR GUITARS ® and certain of its distinctive detailing are registered trademarks of Taylor-Listug, Inc. All Rights Reserved.

About the Author

Erol Ozsever became captivated by the sound of the guitar and began playing at age 10. After witnessing performances from world-renowned guitarists including Christopher Parkening, Manuel Barrueco, and the Romeros, he began studying classical guitar shortly thereafter. His passion for music of all genres has led him on such creative pursuits as rock bands, jazz ensembles, and producing popular music. He holds a Doctor of Music from the Jacobs School of Music at Indiana University. He is a multi-award-winning guitarist and has made numerous radio and television appearances. He has published articles and has given lectures on the psychology of music and motor learning. He has taught classical and popular music at Indiana University and the University of South Florida.

About This Book

Congratulations! Guitar is one of the most fun and rewarding activities out there. But it certainly does not come without its challenges. Strumming and picking require a tremendous amount of motor coordination and can be very frustrating if you try to learn songs that are too difficult too quickly. There are hundreds of guitar methods out there, but here is how this book differs:

We Begin with Chords. The majority of popular songs use guitar to accompany vocals, which means utilizing more chords and strumming to construct the framework of the tune. So you will learn the skills you need to pick up and play your favorite songs right from the start.

Reading chord diagrams is much easier than typical staff notation for the majority of music learners, so you begin playing the songs you want that much more quickly. You will still learn to read musical symbols and notation through these volumes, but at a more gradual pace that doesn't slow you down in the beginning.

Performing riffs or melodies requires significantly more coordination between the two hands, which requires more fine *motor skills*. Strumming is often easier than picking because it is more of a **gross motor skill**, which uses larger muscles and are often easier to develop before **fine**

motor skills used for picking or fingerstyle guitar. While playing chords often involves using more than one finger at a time with the left or fretting hand, your fingers will often move fewer times than if you were playing melodies. This method also includes many chords that are frequently used for popular songs but often omitted from other method books.

Practice Tips

This book does not teach you songs, but rather the chords and skills necessary to play the songs you want to play. There is a myriad of resources available on the web on how to play your favorite songs. This book will equip you with the necessary skills. If you start learning songs that get you excited about playing guitar, you will be that much more motivated to practice, thus you will be much more likely to thrive.

Each exercise in this book is written with a repeat sign. Practice each exercise until each one is smooth before moving on. Try to execute each exercise four times cleanly without stopping. When switching chords **practice slowly.** Practice as slowly as necessary to place each chord accurately. Remember, practice doesn't make perfect if your practice is ridden with mistakes. Mistakes are a normal part of the learning process, but you can greatly reduce the number of mistakes in your practice by taking your time and practicing slowly enough to master the task at hand.

Make sure to **practice often.** Research indicates that practicing daily for shorter periods is more effective than practicing for hours inconsistently[1]. Even if you are crunched for time, even just glancing at the material from your last practice session can be an effective way to refresh your memory. Mental practice is a great technique when picking up the guitar isn't an available option.

Companion tutorial videos for this book are available at:
http://www.ErolOzMusic.com/publications.

---

[1] Erol B. Ozsever, "The Pyschology of Learning for Effective Practice," *Soundboard* 44 no.3 (2018): 10-14.

Introduction

Tuning Pitches

In music we designate notes and chords with the letters A through G. Each guitar string has its own letter name. The letter names of the strings of the guitar from lowest pitch (the thickest string) to highest (thinnest) are: E, A, D, G, B, E.

Or from highest to lowest pitch: E, B, G, D, A, E. For this you can remember: Every-Bad-Guitarist-Does-Awesome-Eventually.
It is also important to note that the high E string is also called the 1st string.

Tuning by ear is a difficult skill that takes time and practice, so as a beginner I highly recommend you purchase either an electronic tuner from your local music store or a guitar tuner app on your smartphone or tablet. Make sure your tuner or app reads 440Hz as this is the standard tuning pitch. If your tuner indicates a ♯ **(sharp)** symbol, the pitch is too high so slowly use the tuning machine to loosen the string. If your tuner indicates a ♭ **(flat)** symbol, gently use the tuning machine to tighten the string.

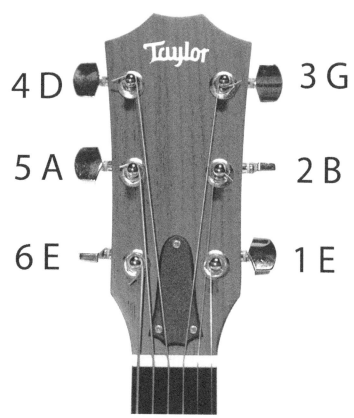

Using a Pick

For beginning guitarists wanting to strum chords, <u>using a pick is optional</u>. Some guitarists find it awkward to hold a pick and choose to strum using the backs of the fingernails. Virtually every guitarist has dealt with shaking a guitar upside down to retrieve lost picks. I have extensive experience in classical guitar, so I only occasionally use a pick when playing acoustic guitar. The majority of classical guitarists use their fingernails to strike the strings. If you choose not to use a pick, <u>try strumming downward with the backs of your fingernails and up with the back of your thumbnail</u>. You may also choose to strum with the flesh of your thumb. Strumming with the flesh of the thumb will produce a delicate sound, but excessive use of this technique can produce a very quiet sound and irritate the skin on your thumb. Strumming with the backs of the nails produces a louder and brighter sound. Additionally, the backs of the fingernails are smoother and produce less friction against the strings and are much less sensitive, so it will often be more comfortable to play this way for extended periods.

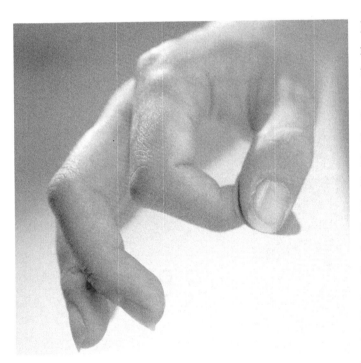

If you choose to use a pick, here is my recommendation. Notice I am cradling the pick against the side of my index finger and keeping it curled in a C-shape. I am not using my index finger to hold to the pick, instead I am using the strength of my thumb, which is much more reliable. I like to hold the pick with what I call an _open grip_, meaning I do not make a fist with my other fingers. Many styles of music use a type of hybrid picking in which guitarists will use a pick for some notes and the remaining digits on the right hand to pluck the higher strings. Additionally, keeping my fingers in this open grip keeps my wrist more relaxed which facilitates better strumming technique.

Strumming Basics

Always focus on strumming more from the wrist than the elbow. Try to keep your movements small and relaxed. When we start playing faster strum patterns, large movements from the elbow will slow you down considerably. Think jazz hands–quick, light, relaxed movements from the wrist.

Tablature

This book focuses predominantly on reading chord diagrams, but **tablature (TAB)** is another style of notating music for guitar and other fretted instruments. There are many tab sites on the web. Many of these sites are user-created, so the most reliable sources are the official published sheet music. Tablature is a relatively straight-forward way to notate guitar music:

- a set of six horizontal lines represent the strings of the guitar.
- The top line represents the 1st string or the high E, and the bottom line represents the 6th string or the low E.
- numbers on the lines which represent which frets to press on the indicated string.

Here is an example of tablature:

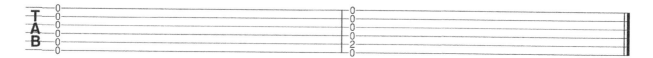

Notice in the first example we have six 0's stacked vertically. When we have multiple numbers stacked and aligned vertically, it means that we strum all numbered strings together.

In the second example, there is a number 2 on the 2nd line from the bottom. This means that we will press that string (the 5th A string) at the 2nd fret. Notice all other strings are 0's which indicate to strum open strings. Press the A (5th) string at the 2nd fret and strum all six strings. This is our first chord, called E minor 7. On the following page we you will see a detailed chord diagram and photos of how to play this chord.

For a video tutorial on reading tablature, visit http://www.ErolOzMusic.com/publications.

Good Luck!

Now it's time to turn the page and get started!

Reading Chord Diagrams

This symbol indicates to strum in a downward motion

This diamond-shaped note is a whole note. Whole notes last for four counts. Strum the strings and count steadily to four.

The chord diagram below represents a vertical orientation of the fingerboard of the guitar.

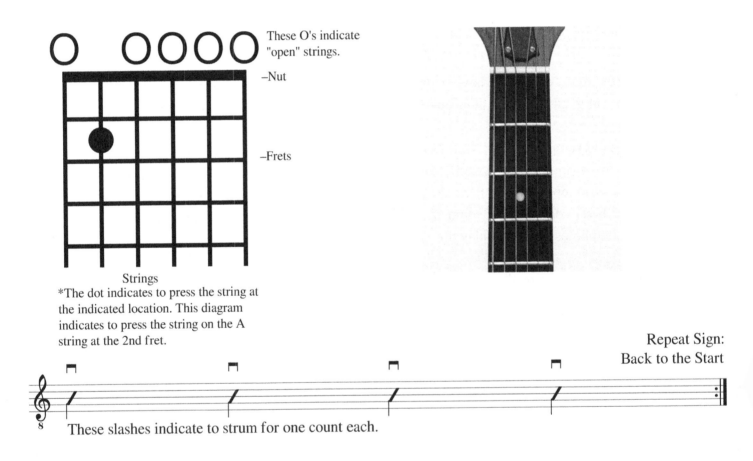

These O's indicate "open" strings.

–Nut

–Frets

Strings

*The dot indicates to press the string at the indicated location. This diagram indicates to press the string on the A string at the 2nd fret.

Repeat Sign:
Back to the Start

These slashes indicate to strum for one count each.

Eminor⁷

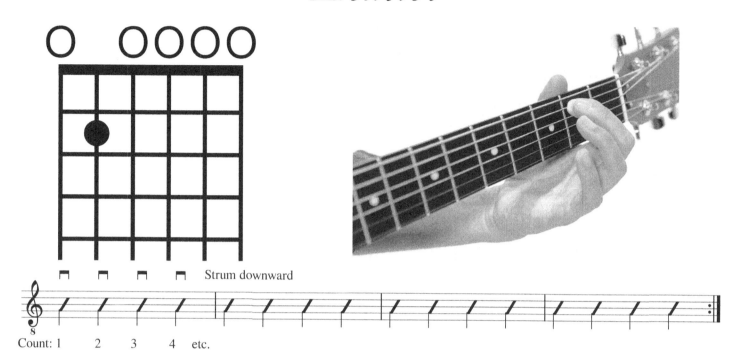

Strum downward

Count: 1   2   3   4   etc.

Eminor

8

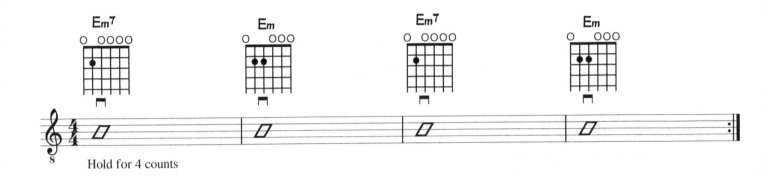

Hold for 4 counts

1   rest   rest   rest

1   2   rest   rest

1   2   3   rest

1   2   3   4

A⁷ chord

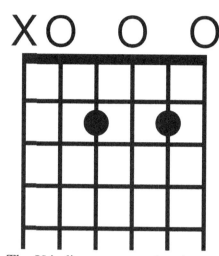

The X indicates not to play that particular string. You can use your left thumb to lightly rest on the low E string to mute the sound. Most people find this is easier than strumming only five of the six strings.

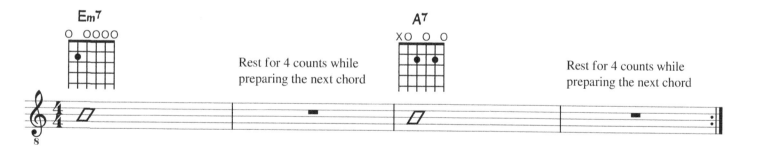

Em⁷

Rest for 4 counts while preparing the next chord

A⁷

Rest for 4 counts while preparing the next chord

*8th Notes are played twice as fast as quarter notes.

D⁶ chord

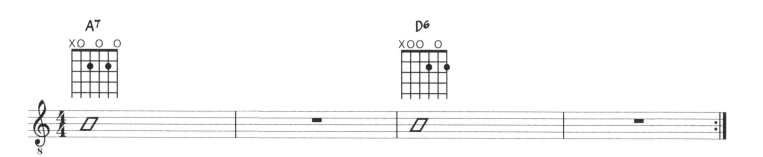

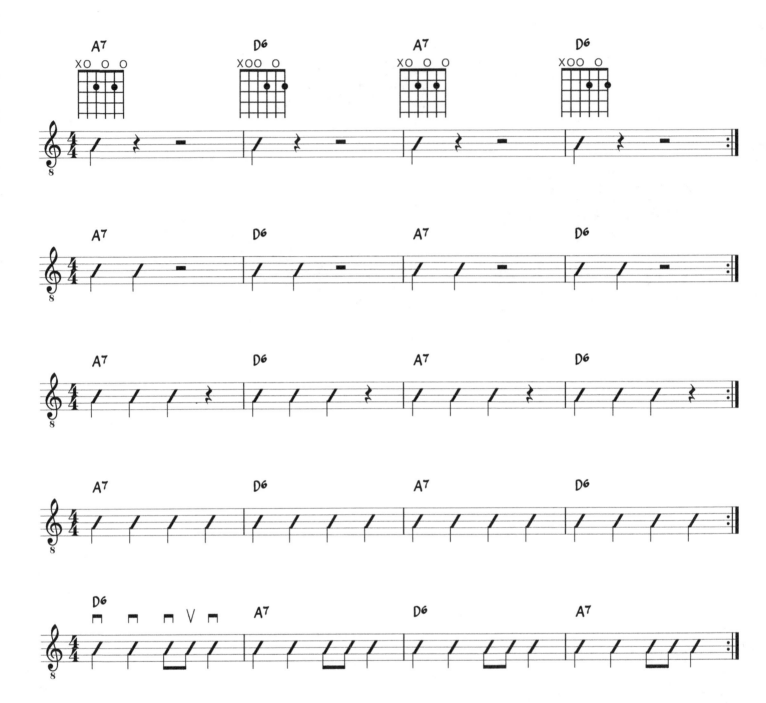

D

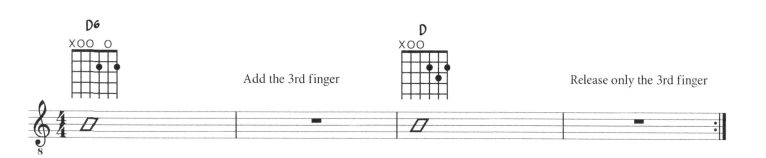

D6 — Add the 3rd finger

D — Release only the 3rd finger

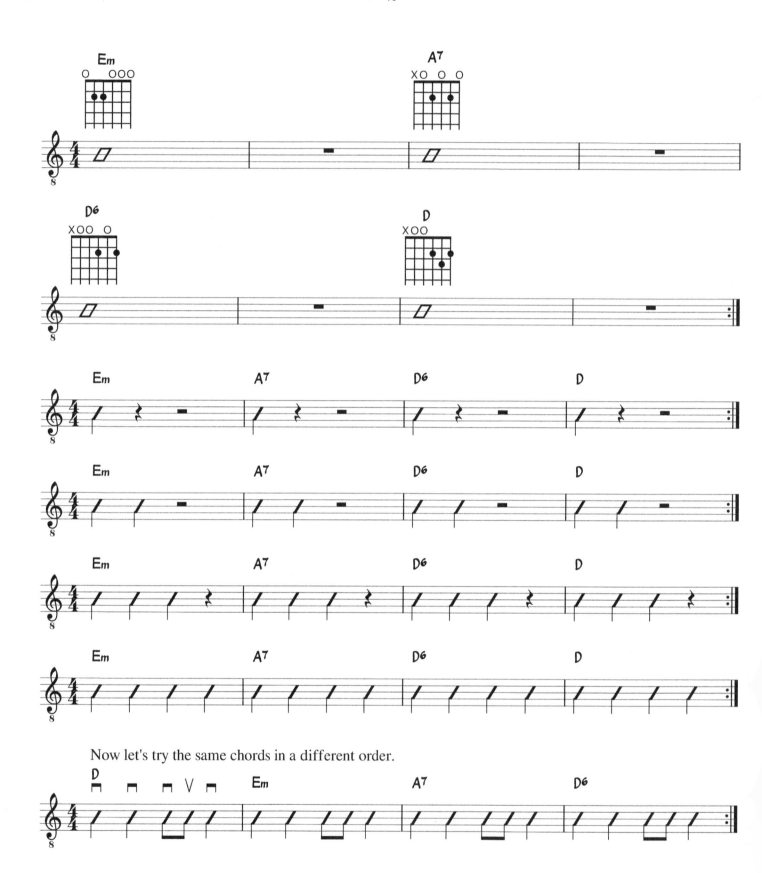

Now let's try the same chords in a different order.

Dsus⁴

D

Simply add the 4th finger to the D chord so all 4 fingers are pressing into the fretboard

Dsus⁴

Simply release the 4th finger

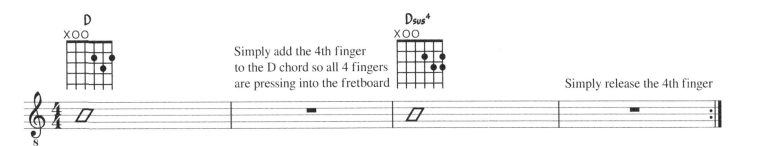

D

Try to move the 1st and 2nd fingers as a group rather than individually

A⁷

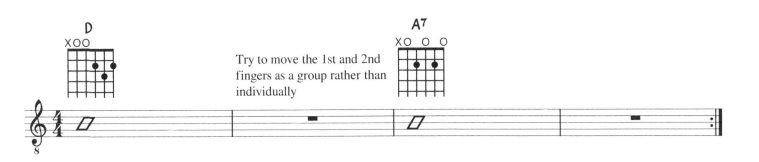

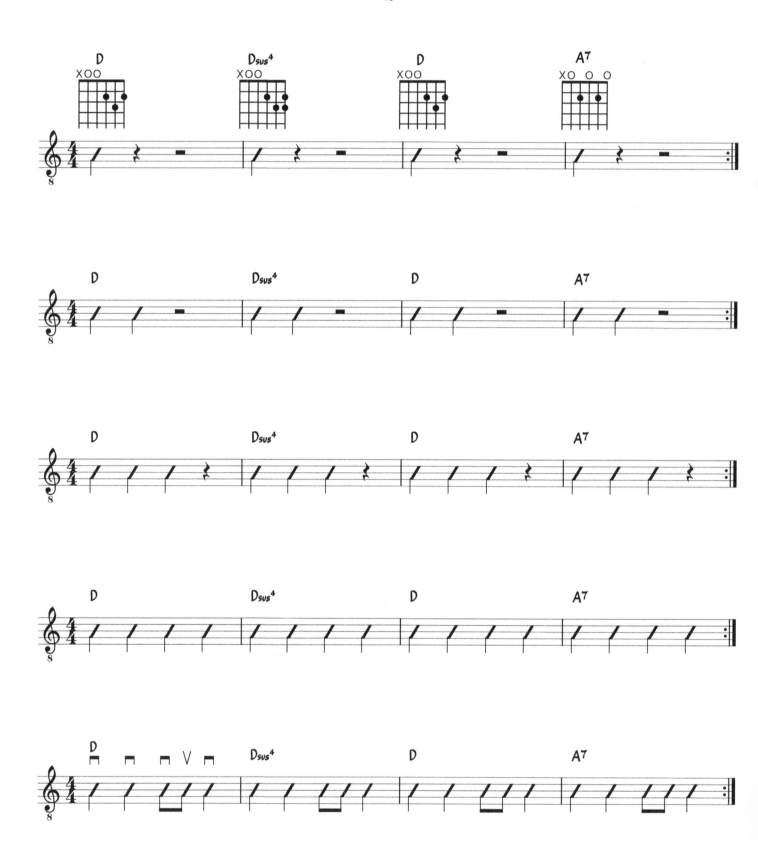

G

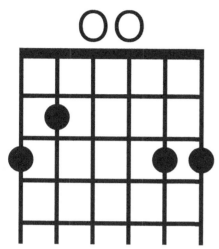

G is one of the most commonly used chords in popular music. There are many acceptable fingerings for a G chord, but this one is used very commonly in modern popular songs.

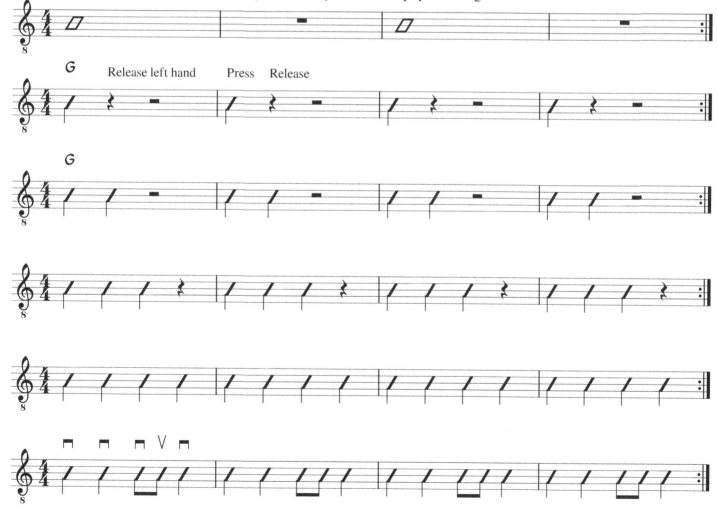

Leave your 3rd and 4th fingers down while moving the 1st & 2nd fingers

21

Cadd9

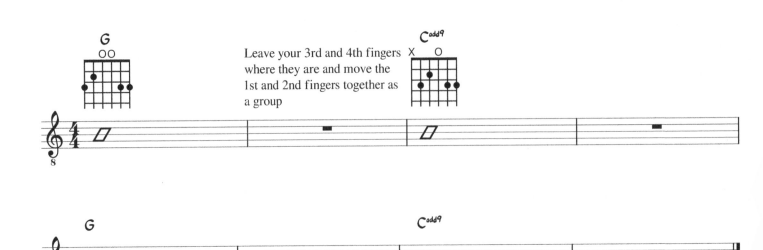

Leave your 3rd and 4th fingers where they are and move the 1st and 2nd fingers together as a group

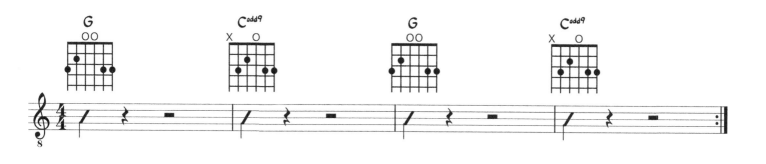

Aminor⁷

Am

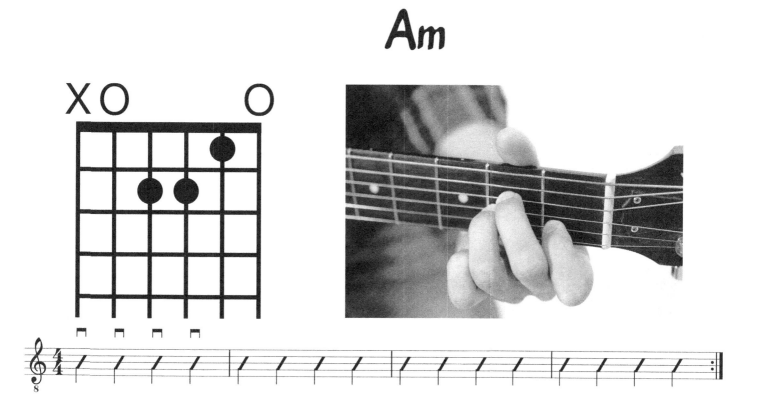

C

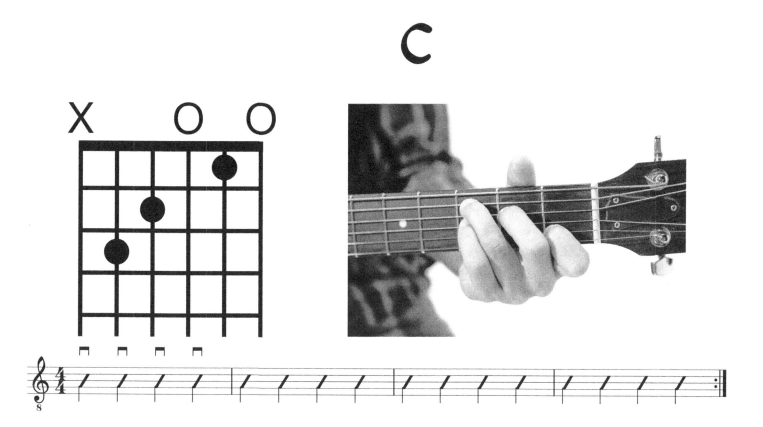

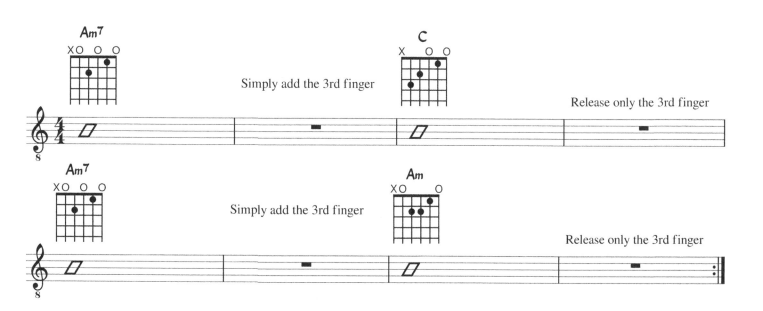

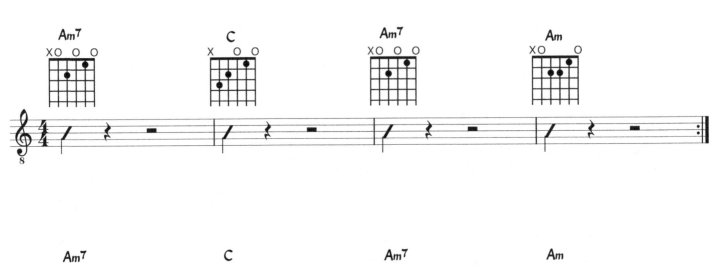

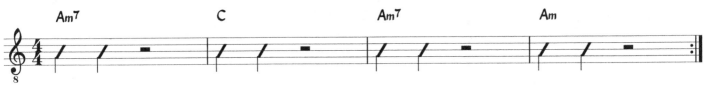

E

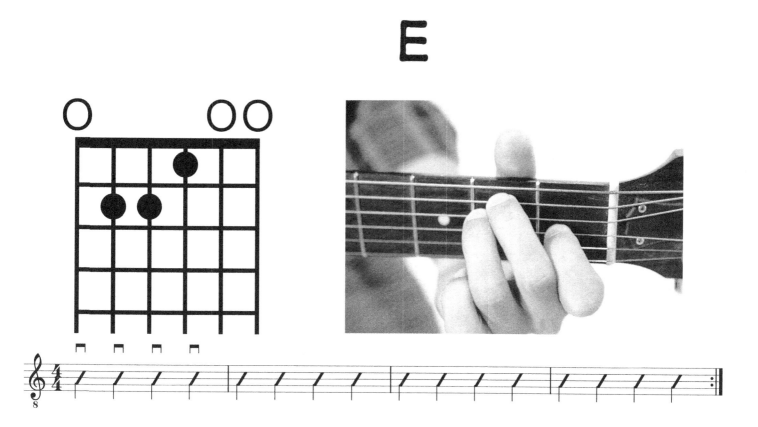

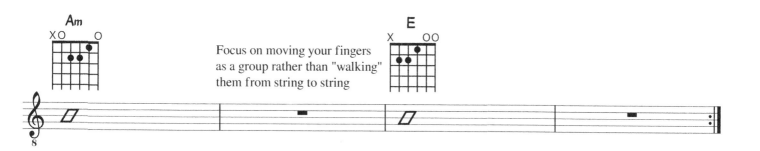

Focus on moving your fingers
as a group rather than "walking"
them from string to string

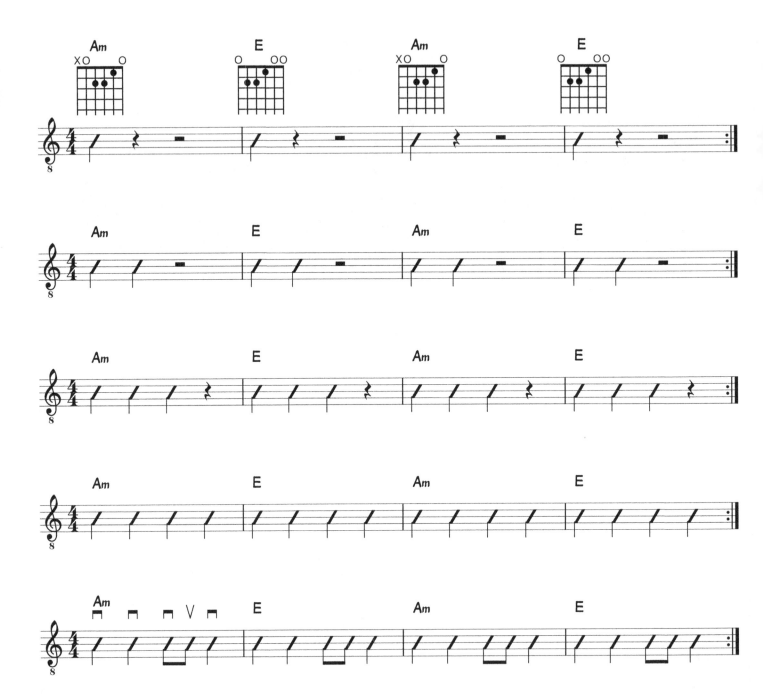

FMajor⁷

Leave your 1st and 3rd fingers down, move your 2nd finger to the adjacent string, and add the 4th finger to the 4th string. Since this is a complex comound movement, practice as slowly as necessary for accurate placement.

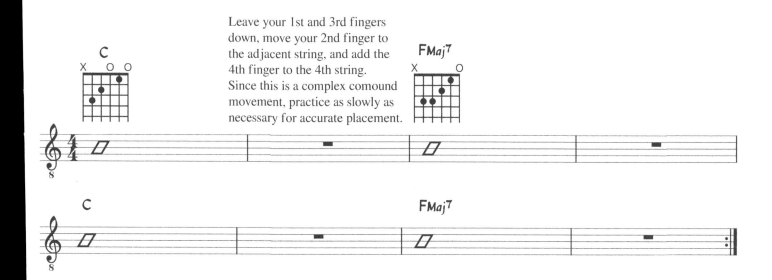

Additional Strum Patterns

*Notice in each exercise that when we count numbered beats we strum downward and upward on the &'s.

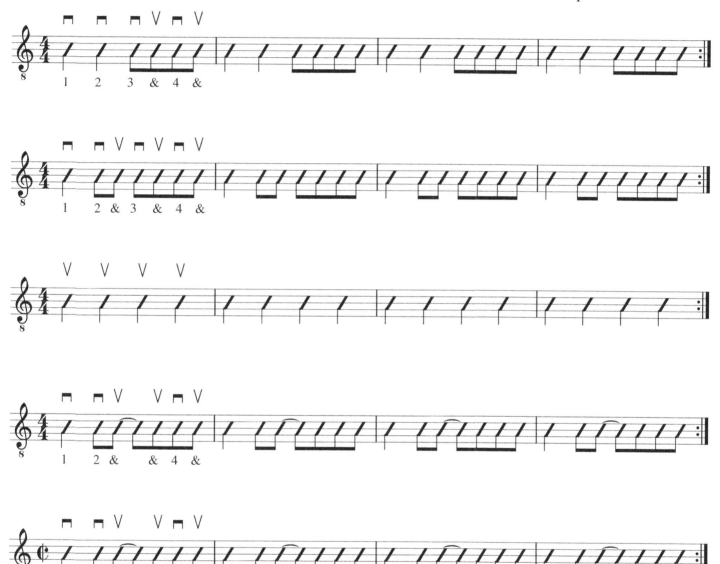

*Notice this example is not in 4/4 time. It is in cut time, which has a double-time feel from 4/4. In order to be able to strum this quickly, make sure to keep the movements in your wrist light, relaxed, and small. Large, swinging movements from the elbow will slow you down and give you a noisy tone.

Chord Progessions

Chord progressions are sequences of chords that are used to play popular songs. One of the most common chord progressions is called a I-IV-V chord progressions, or 1-4-5. Simply put, our 1 chord is based on the key of the song and is most often our starting point for a chord progression.

Notice the example below. The first chord is a G chord, so we identify it as the I (1) chord.

We then call the C chord the IV (4) chord because it is the fourth note in the key of G. We then call D the V (5) chord because it is built from the fifth note in the key of G.

I-IV-V chord progressions have been used in every style of western music from hymns to folk to pop to rock. The following unit will have you playing the following chord progressions in a varity of keys:

I-IV-V: Commonly used in virtually every style of western music
I-vi-IV-V: Commonly used in pop music
I-V-vi-IV: Commonly used in modern pop and rock
I-vi-ii-V: Common used in early jazz standards

Notice that the ii and the vi chords are notated using lower-case numerals. This indicates that these will be minor chords. These same chords can be identified with Arabic numerals, which is derived from what is commonly known as the Nashville Number System, which I recommend for further reading.

The follow chart represents the chords used for several common keys using Roman numerals:

I	ii	iii	IV	V	vi	vii°*
G	Am	Bm	C	D	Em	F#diminished
D	Em	F#m	G	A	Bm	C#dim
C	Dm	Em	F	G	Am	Bdim
A	Bm	C#m	D	E	F#m	G#dim
E	F#m	G#m	A	B	C#m	D#dim

* Diminished chords are used less commonly in popular music.
It is important to note that not every song will follow this pattern and structure, though many will.
We will take a more in-depth look at keys and sharps in the Music Theory for Songwriters volume.

I - IV - V in G

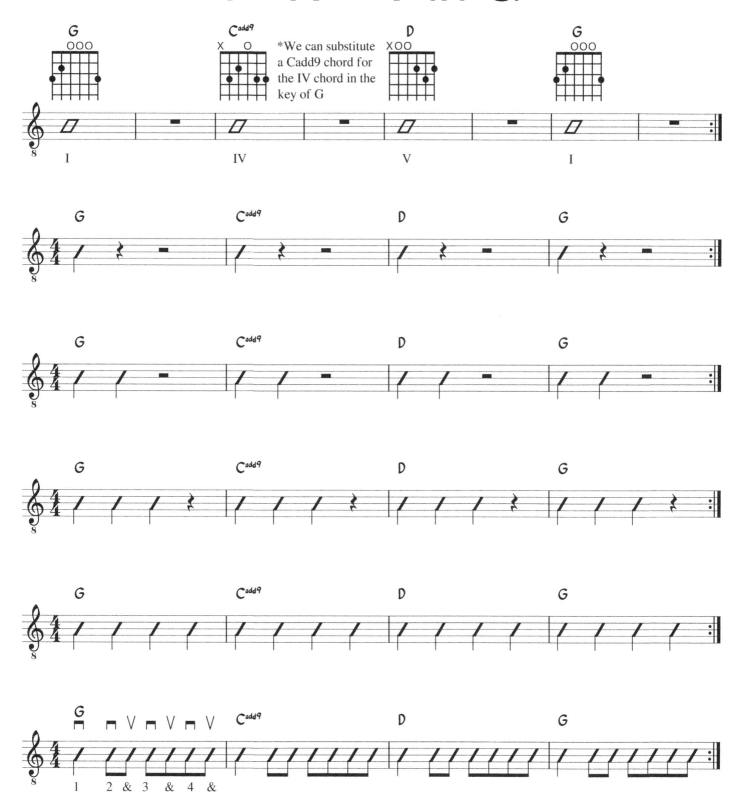

*We can substitute a Cadd9 chord for the IV chord in the key of G

I - IV - V in G

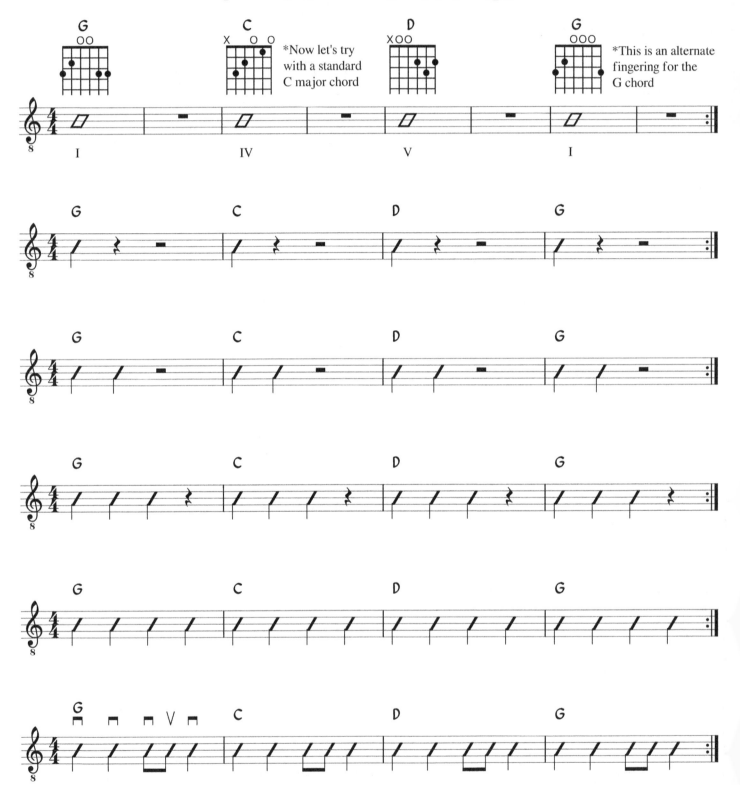

I - IV - V in D

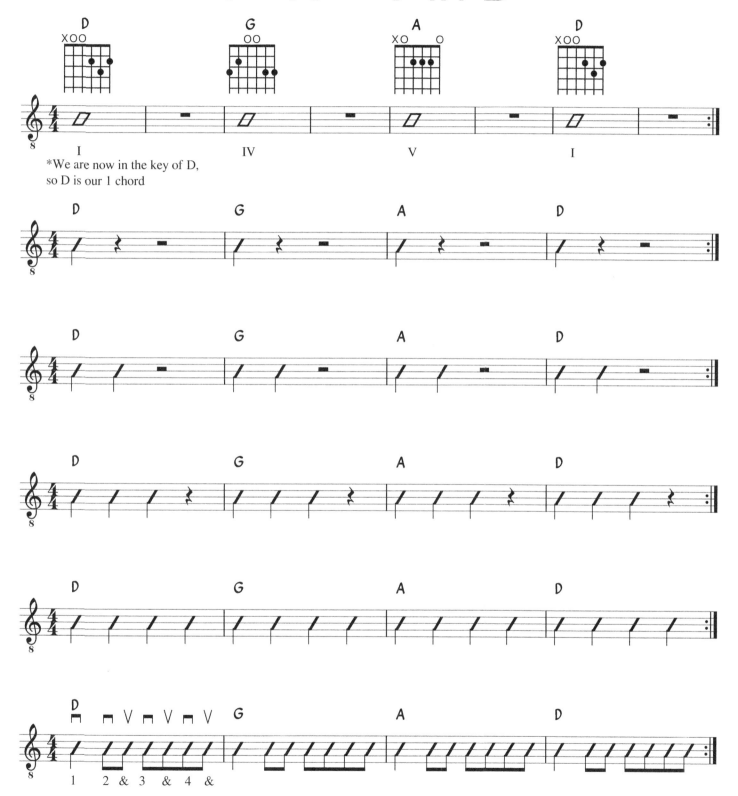

*We are now in the key of D,
so D is our 1 chord

I - IV - V in A

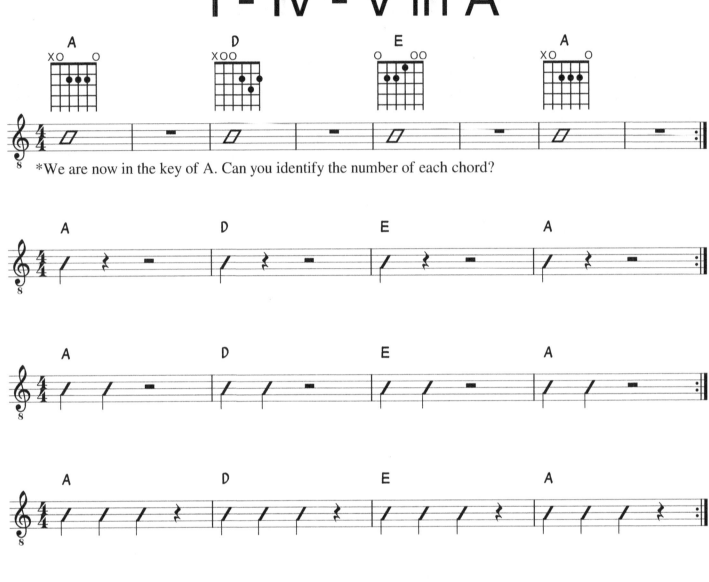

*We are now in the key of A. Can you identify the number of each chord?

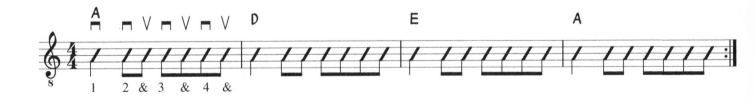

I - IV - V in C

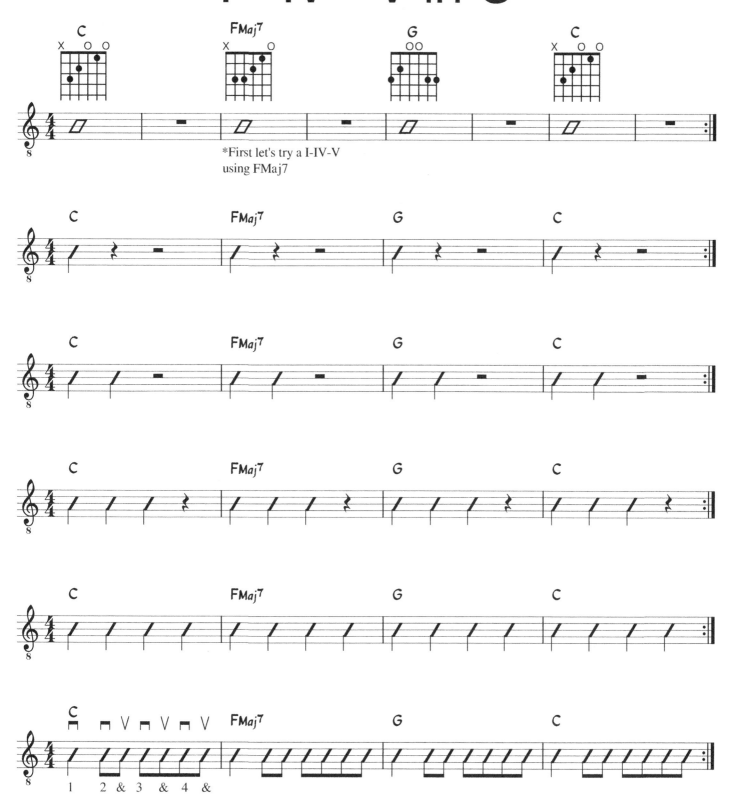

*First let's try a I-IV-V
using FMaj7

I - IV - V in E

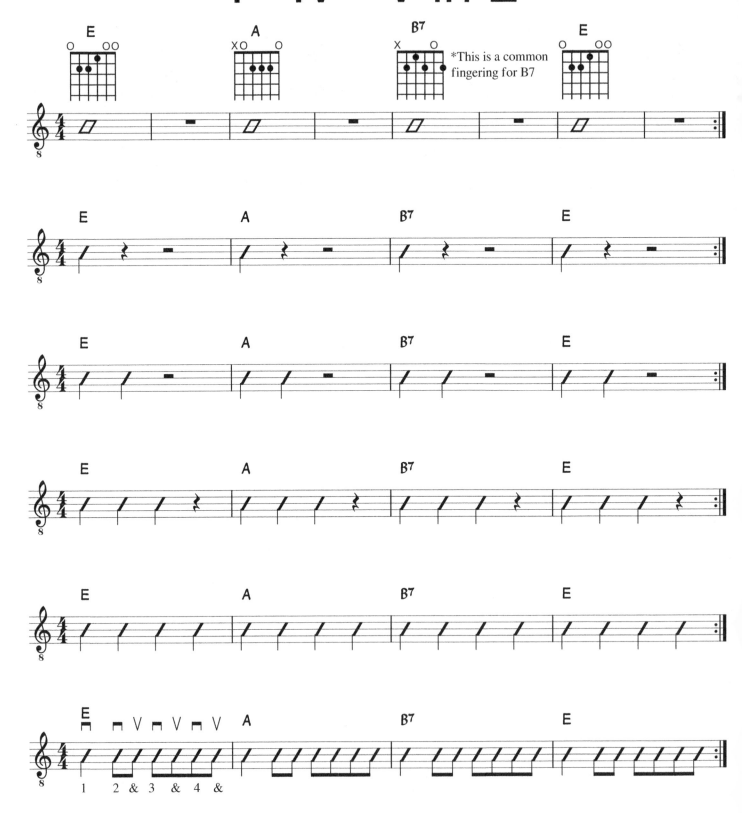

*This is a common fingering for B7

Blues

A7

This chord progression is an example of 12-BAR-BLUES because there are 12 measures (bars) in the pattern. There are innumerable songs that use this pattern from blues to early jazz to early rock & roll. In order to play a 12-bar blues, we will often use 7th chords, which are often called DOMINANT 7th chords. We need a I chord, a IV chord, and a V chord in the key of our song.

I

*Note the fingering of D7 instead of D

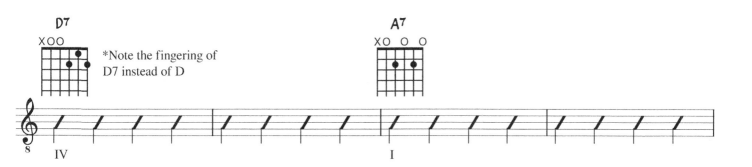

IV   I

*Use fingers 1 & 2

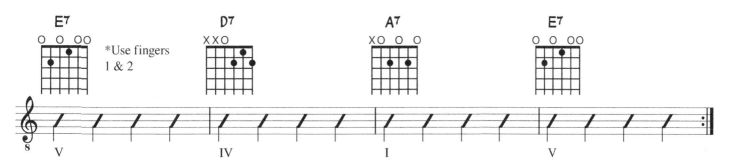

V   IV   I   V

There are many variations on a 12-bar blues. This is the most basic form of the pattern, but you may encounter some of these variations as you continue to learn your favorite songs.

Barre (Bar) Chords

Certain chords will require you hold down multiple strings with a single finger. This technique is called **barring**. Barre chords are challenging for beginners, but they are frequently used for virtually all styles of music. In order to get a clean sound from your barre chords, you will need to place your thumb in the middle of the back of the neck underneath your middle finger. If your left thumb starts to feel sore or tired, simply release the chord and allow your left hand to fall at your side and relax. Do not over-stretch your thumb as this may make the soreness worse.

F

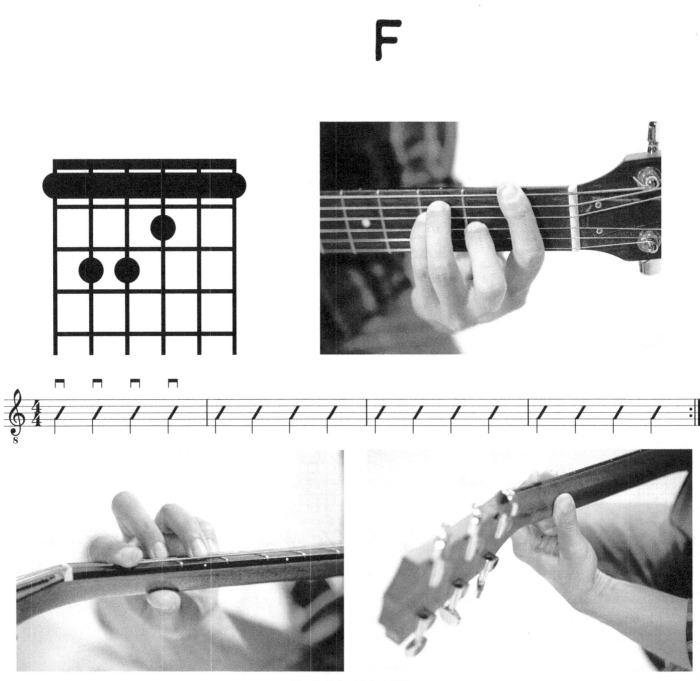

In order to transition into barre chords more easily, let's start by revisiting the FMajor7 chord. Once placing the 2nd, 3rd, & 4th fingers feel easy, it makes adding the barre less challenging. For many guitarists, focusing on placing the barre first can slow you down.

FMajor⁷

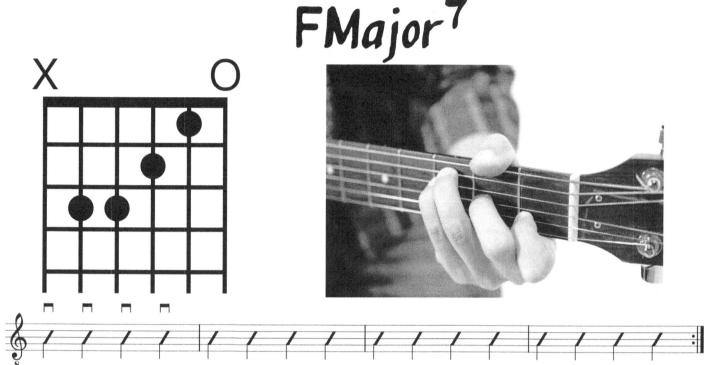

Now release your first finger and lay it flat across all six strings. These are called BARRE (bar) chords.

F

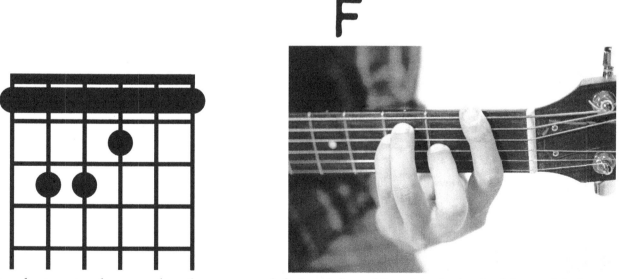

In order to get a clear sound, make sure your left thumb is positioned in the back of the neck below your 2nd finger. Thumb placement is key to getting optimum grip strength from your barre chords.

F⁷

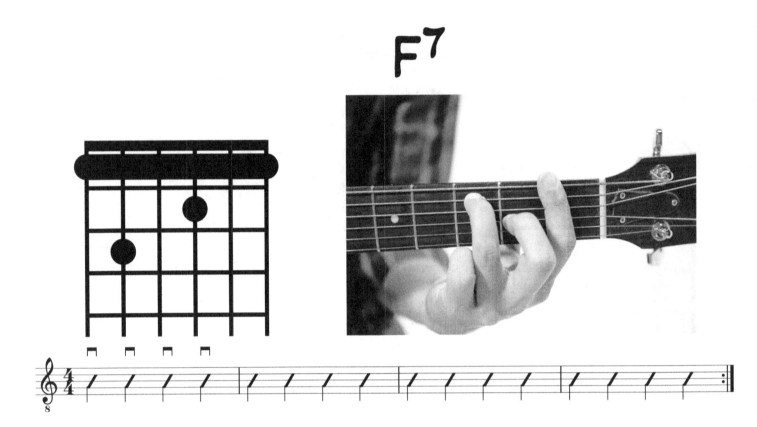

Fm

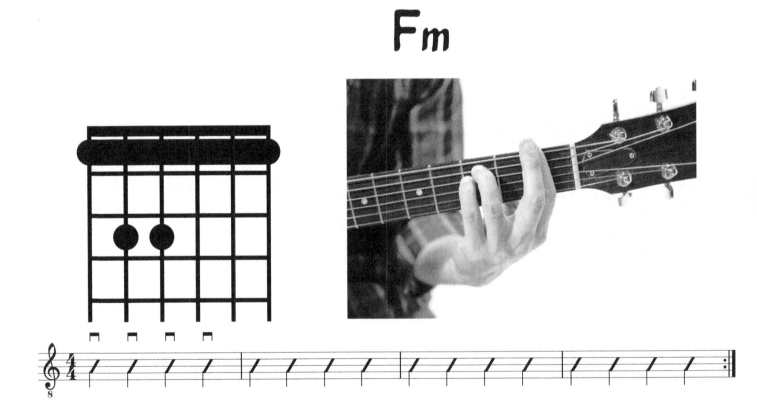

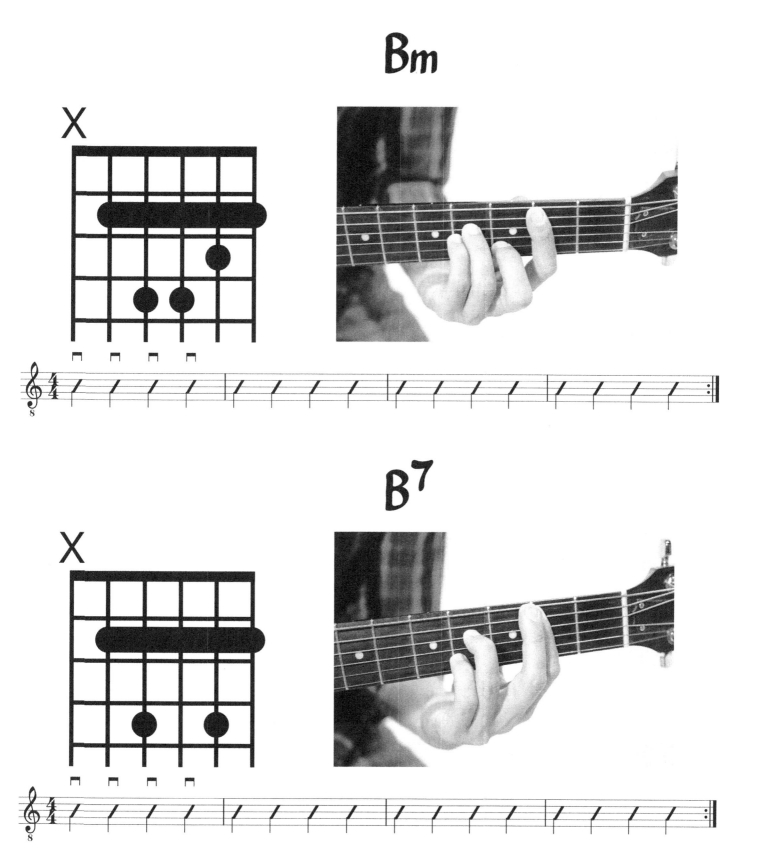

Bm

B⁷

I - vi - IV - V in G

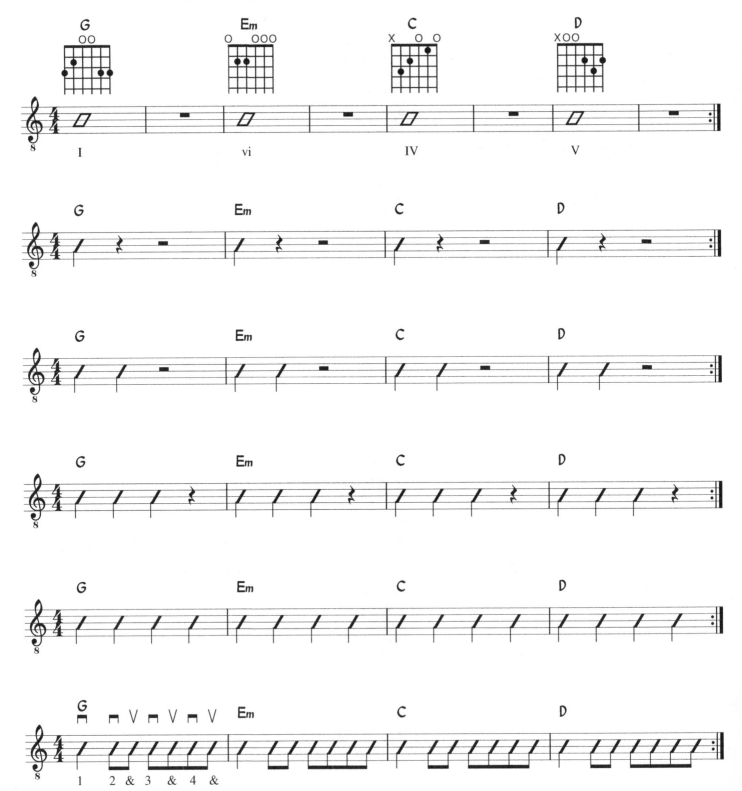

I - V - vi - IV in G

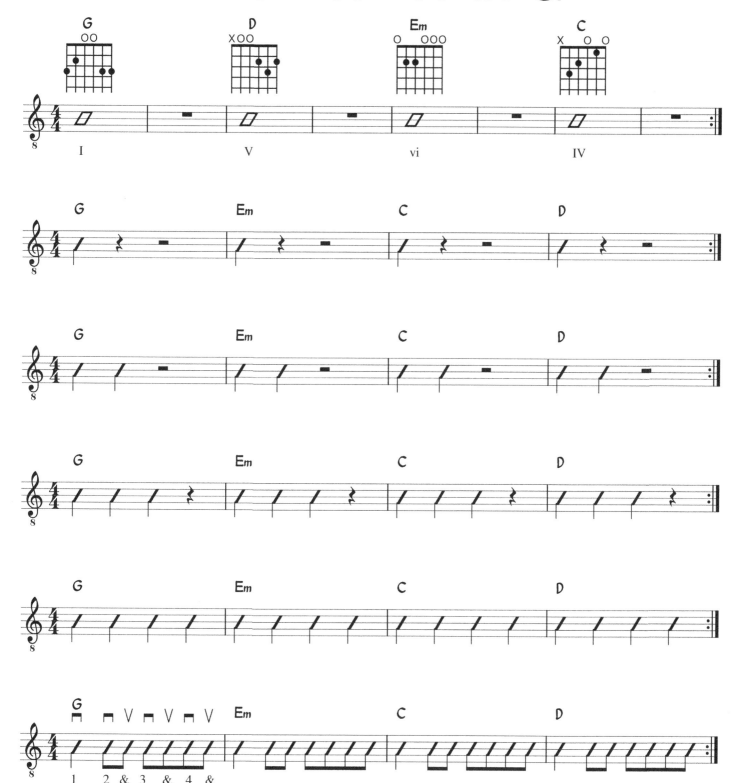

I – vi – ii – V in G

I - V - vi - IV in D

I - vi - ii - V in D

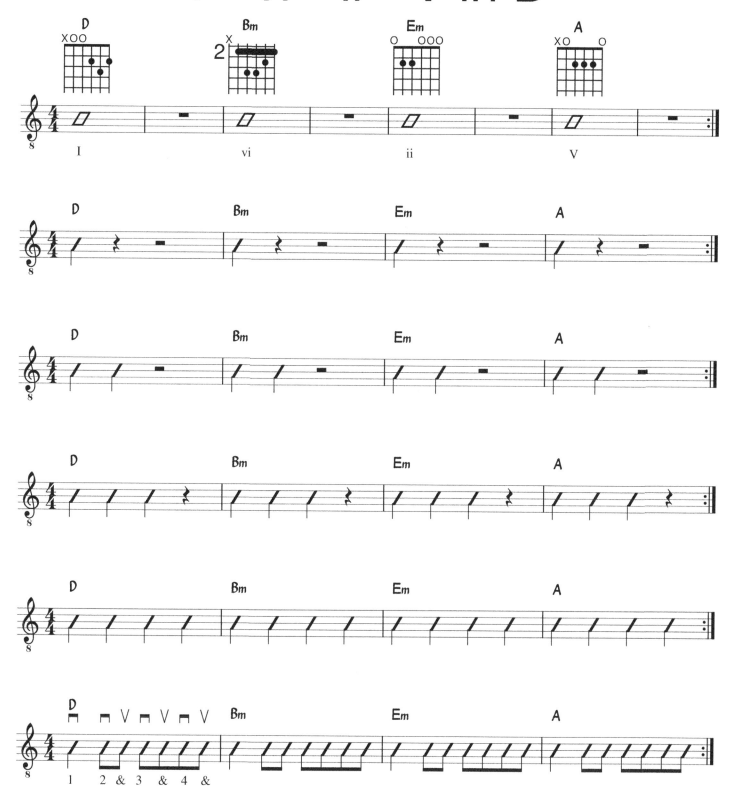

I - vi - IV - V in A

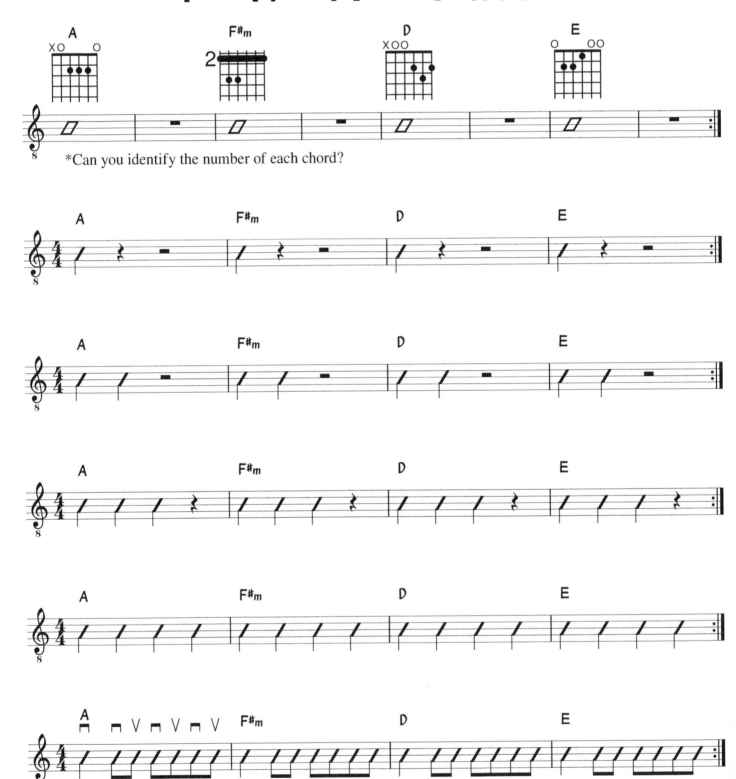

*Can you identify the number of each chord?

I - V - vi - IV in A

I - vi - ii - V in A

I - vi - IV - V in C

I - V - vi - IV in C

I – vi – ii – V in C

Chord Progressions in C

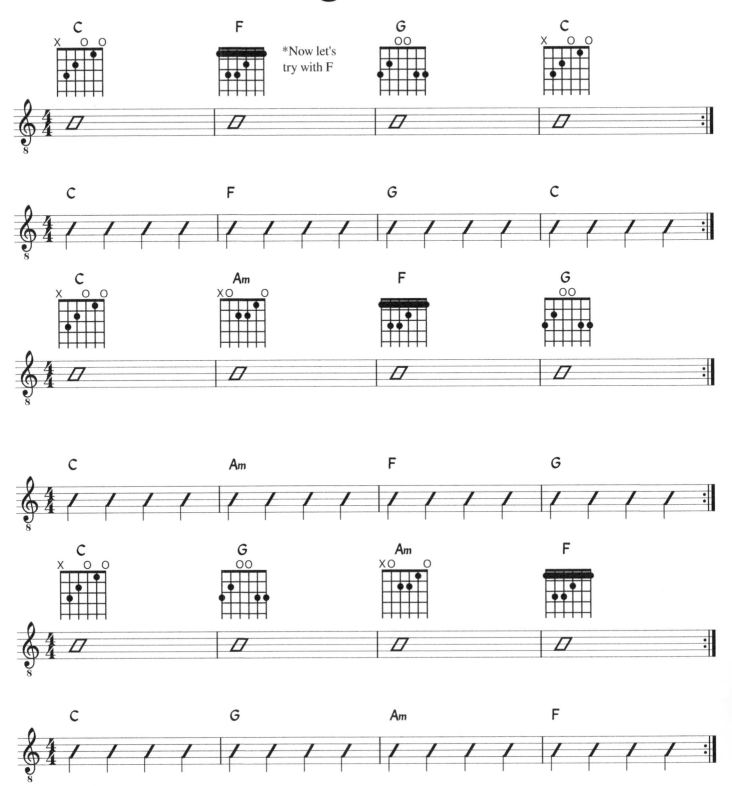

*Now let's try with F

I - vi - IV - V in E

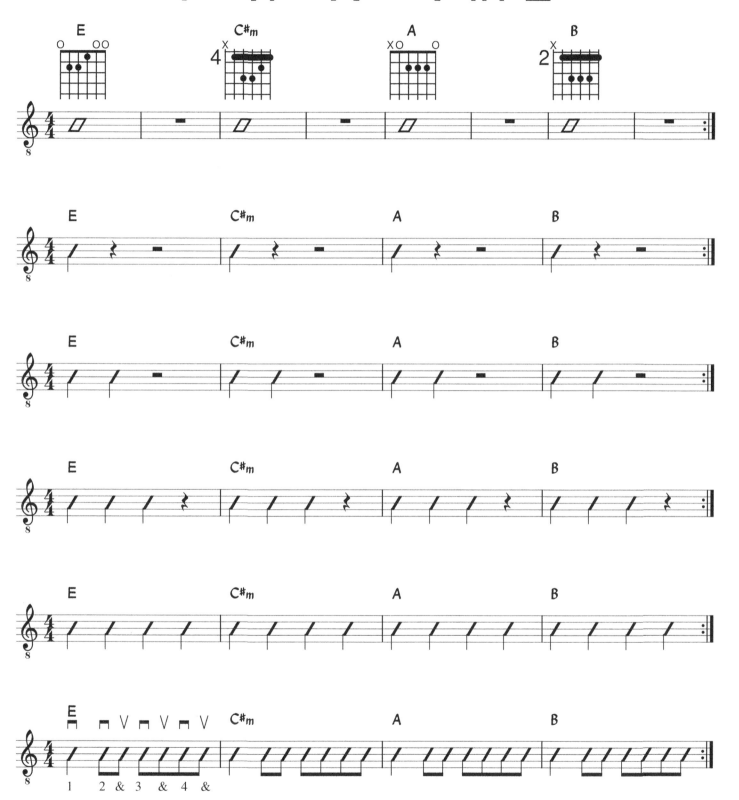

I - V - vi - IV in E

I – vi – ii – V in E

Chord Finder

*Denotes an alternate fingering for the chord.

Made in the USA
Coppell, TX
15 September 2022

83070230R00037